Bodies Fins and Stripes

CONTENTS

NATIONAL GEOGRAPHIC   Hampton-Brown

School Publishing

Words with y

Look at each picture. Read the words.

Example:

ba**y**

fl**y**

stud**y**

tin**y**

cit**y**

sk**y**

High Frequency
Words

animal
color
group
might
most
move

Key Words

Read the sets of sentences.
Match each set to a picture.

red fox

ants

Which One?

Set A

1. This **animal** has a **color** in its name.

2. You **might** see it by its den.

3. It hides **most** of the time.

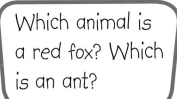
Which animal is a red fox? Which is an ant?

Set B

1. This animal lives in a **group**.

2. It is very strong.

3. It can **move** big things for its size.

Phonics Games
NGReach.com

Not the Same

by Dee Wallis

kangaroo

wallaby

Some animals might look or act the same. But these animals are not quite the same.

Study each group of animals. Try to see which one is not the same.

These animals are birds. Most can fly, but one can not. Which one?

emu

An emu can move fast on land. It runs on long legs. But you will not see it in the sky!

These tiny animals are bugs. Which
one is very, very strong for its size?

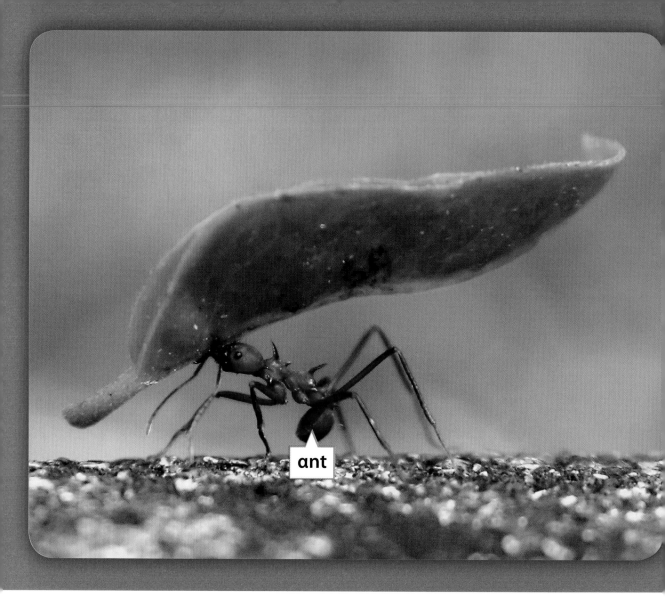

ant

A tiny ant is strong. It can move things
that are fifty times its weight! Can you?

These animals are fish. They can all
swim. But one can walk, too! Which one?

catfish

This kind of catfish can walk on land.
Its fins are like legs. They move the
fish's body.

These animals live in the same place. They all move. Which one moves less than the others?

sloth

The sloth does not move much. It hangs from a branch and is still for a long time. It must be cozy up there! ❖

Words with <u>y</u>

Read these words.

baby	fly	lucky	tiny
body	huge	strong	key

Find the words with **y**.
Use letters to build them.

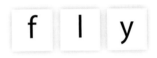

Talk Together

Choose words from the box above to tell your partner about the animal and her baby.

Her <u>body</u> is <u>huge</u>.

Plurals -s, -es, -ies

Look at the pictures. See how plurals are made. Read the words.

ape

ape

ap**es**

fox

fox

fox**es**

pupp **ies**

y

puppy

pupp**ies**

High Frequency
Words

High Frequency Words
animal
color
group
might
most
move

Key Words

Look at the picture.
Read the sentences.

Find the Male

1. Can you spot the male **animal** in the **group**?
2. The male animal **might** be big.
3. He might have the **most** **color**.
4. He might **move** fast.

Which animal is the male?

GO! **Phonics Games**

NGReach.com

15

Male Animals

by Kelsey Bruce

male

female

babies

Animal babies are cute! Their mom is a female. Their dad is a male.

The male and female do not always look like each other.

Can you tell which animals are male?

These are lions. Which is the male?

mane

The male lion is the one with the mane. The mane makes the lion look very big.

These are apes. Which is the male?

The male ape is the big one. Most
male apes are too big to move through
trees. But females can!

These are ducks. Which is the male?

The male duck is the one with all the colors. The female duck might blend in with the pond. But you can see the male duck because of his colors.

eggs

Frogs hatch masses of eggs. This frog is sitting on eggs. Is it male or female?

babies

It's a male! His job is to sit on the
eggs, so they don't get dry. When they
hatch, the babies ride on his back. ❖

Plurals -s, -es, -ies

Read these words.

babies	bus	dogs	kiss	spots
boxes	cats	finches	puppies	stripes

Find the plurals.
Use letters to build them.

b o x e s

Talk Together

Choose words from
the box above to
tell your partner
about the animals
in the pet shop.

The __cats__ have __babies__.

25

Arctic Animals

Some animals like cold, snowy places.
Take turns reading the clues with a partner.
Find the animals.

1 This animal is just one color.

2 This animal can fly.

3 These animals like to move in a group.

4 These babies might have the most fun on ice!

5 This animal has big tusks.

6 These animals like the tiny patches of plants.

Acknowledgments

Grateful acknowledgment is given to the authors, artists, photographers, museums, publishers, and agents for permission to reprint copyrighted material. Every effort has been made to secure the appropriate permission. If any omissions have been made or if corrections are required, please contact the Publisher.

Photographic Credits

CVR (c) Richard Carey/iStockphoto. (l) Alexander Hafemann/iStockphoto. (r) Henk Bentlage/iStockphoto. **2** (bl) DigitalStock/Corbis. (br) Eyewire. (cl) quavondo/iStockphoto. (cr) Brandon Laufenberg/iStockphoto. (tl) Ana Abejon/iStockphoto. (tr) Creatas/Jupiterimages. **3** (b) Liz Garza Williams/Hampton-Brown/National Geographic School Publishing. (l) PureStock/SuperStock. (r) Paul Erickson/iStockphoto. **4** (l) PhotoDisc/Getty Images. (r) Eric Isselée/iStockphoto. **5** (bl) mikeuk/iStockphoto. (br) james steidl/iStockphoto. (tl) Frank Leung/iStockphoto. (tr) Nicola Stratford/iStockphoto. **6** Daniel Gangur/Shutterstock. **7** (bl) Nekan/iStockphoto. (br) Chepko Danil/iStockphoto. (tl) pixelmaniak/iStockphoto. (tr) Satoshi Kuribayashi/Oxford Scientific (OSF)/Photolibrary. **8** Jacom Stephens/iStockphoto. **9** (bl) Digital Vision/Getty Images. (br) Reinhard Dirscherl/WaterFrame - Underwater Images/Photolibrary. (tl) Mella Panzella/Animals Animals. (tr) Grant Klotz/Alaskastock/Photolibrary. **10** Robert Sisson/National Geographic Image Collection. **11** (bl) Gerald Hoberman/Hoberman Collection UK/Photolibrary. (br) Juan Carlos Muñoz/age fotostock/Photolibrary. (tl) PureStock/SuperStock. (tr) Neil Hinds/iStockphoto. **12** Michael & Patricia Fogden/Corbis. **13** (l) Ronald van der Beek/Shutterstock. (r) Liz Garza Williams/Hampton-Brown/National Geographic School Publishing. **14** (bl) Stephaniellen/Shutterstock. (br) Shane Wilson Link/Shutterstock. (cl) Ronnie Howard/Shutterstock. (cr) Northof60/iStockphoto. (tl) Digital Vision/Getty Images. (tr) Polka Dot Images/Jupiterimages. **15** (b) Liz Garza Williams/Hampton-Brown/National Geographic School Publishing. (t) Michael Ventura/Alamy Images. **16** Benson HE/Shutterstock. (inset) Ken Araujo/Photographer's Direct. **17** DigitalStock/Corbis. **18** Alan D. Carey/PhotoDisc/Getty Images. **19** Elvele Images Ltd/Alamy Images. **20** Nicole Aletta Planken-Kooij/iStockphoto. **21** Terry Alexander/Shutterstock. **22** Frank Leung/iStockphoto. **23** Neil Bromhall/Nature Picture Library. **24** Kevin Schafer/Alamy Images. **25** (l) Liz Garza Williams/Hampton-Brown/National Geographic School Publishing.

Illustrator Credits

14 Peter Grosshauser. **25, 26-27** Stevie Mahardhika

The National Geographic Society

John M. Fahey, Jr., President & Chief Executive Officer
Gilbert M. Grosvenor, Chairman of the Board

National Geographic School Publishing
Hampton-Brown
www.NGSP.com

Printed in the USA.
RR Donnelley, Jefferson City, MO

ISBN: 978-0-7362-8039-6

12 13 14 15 16 17 18 19
10 9 8 7 6 5 4

New High Frequency Words

animal
color
group
might
most
move

Target Sound/Spellings

Words with -y	Plurals -s, -es, -ies
Selection: **Not the Same**	**Selection:** **Male Animals**
body	apes
cozy	babies
fifty	ducks
fly	eggs
sky	frogs
study	masses
tiny	pages
try	